Love for Haiti

Robin Tina Duckrey Moore

To order additional copies of this book, contact:
Xlibris
844-714-8691
www.Xlibris.com
Orders@Xlibris.com

ISBN: Softcover   978-1-4535-6031-0
                 EBook   979-8-3694-0624-3

Print information available on the last page

Rev. date: 08/23/2023

HAITI

H-Hope- future-Health Opportunity for the people

A- Above a higher place than before

I-Improvement for improvement

T- Time and action for the project

I- Incense and fragrance for the odor to make a perfume smell.

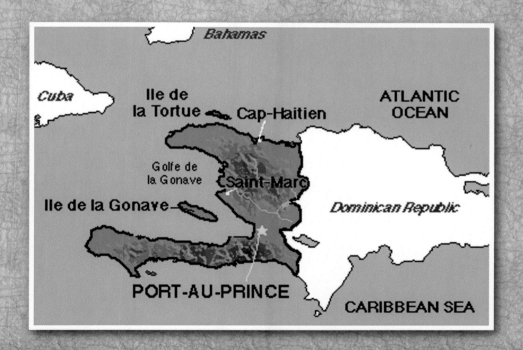

LOVE

L- Living to live again

O-Only one amazing love is God's he will never stop loving you

V- Very special people

E- Encouragement to help others

REMEMBER

Jesus is on the front line all the time

GOD

God is there for Haiti. God came down on earth for Haiti and went underground and blew his breath underground so the people could inhale and exhale the air he gave to save lives. That was a miracle that only God could do. He also gave light where they needed light. Haiti, God cares for you and he knows your pain. In time the healing will take place. Only by God's grace, mercy, love and hope for all God's children Haiti is still standing.

LIFE

When a tragedy like this happens it hurts everyone. So we cry and pray to God that he will lead us on the path way to life, understanding and good will to man.

HARVEST TIME

Haiti this is your season to grow seed, plant, and water. Haiti, the world is healing with you in your season of harvest time.

LOVE FOR HAITI

HISTORY

Generation after Generation will talk about this earthquake all over the world. They will help Haiti in every way they can. This is an on going healing full of love.

WISDOM

Haiti does not take to heart everything that you hear some people saying because they do not know what they say. So while you are going through recovery, stay wise and have wisdom and strength to get through this.

LOVE FOR HAITI

HEAVEN

H- Healing for the people of Haiti

E- Every lasting love

A-Above the will of God

V- Victory is Haiti's people

E- Eternal Life

N- Not below, but above

Moore, Robin Tina Duckrey

SEED

The seed has been planted like flowing water for the plant, giving it the nutrition and light. That is what is happening for Haiti new life.

FLAG

HAITI THE RED WHITE AND BLUE IS BEHIND YOU

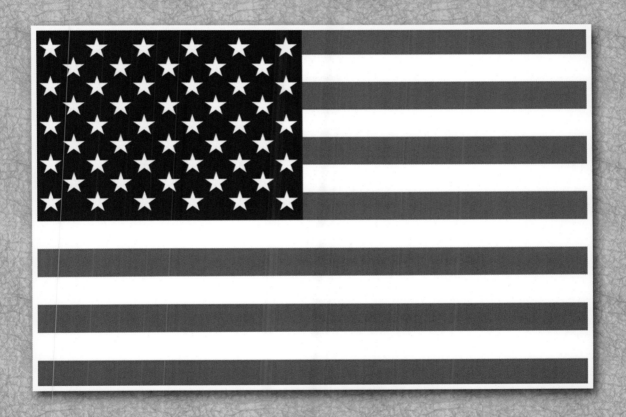

HAITI SPITE OF

Numerous set backs, challenges and death's disappointments, you are still praising the Lord. That's why you are being blessed in so many ways

LOVE FOR HAITI

SAVIOR

When there is no one to talk to, nowhere to go, and nowhere to turn, you can always turn to God.

UNITY

The promise land is what Haiti showed the world. Love, hope, joy, freedom and caring about others. Peace of mine, unity, faith, strength, and belief. Thank you for blessing the world Haiti for your Obedience to God's words.

HARD BALL

Sometimes life throws you a hardball. You have to be able to get up and believe God will get you through it, like he did before. So make the best of what you have because it only going to get better in time. You can't keep a good man, woman or country down.

COVER BY THE BLOOD

Haiti, all of your needs are being meet. God made it so the world will be there for Haiti. So do not worry about anything. God covers Haiti with his blood and put his hands all around the land of Haiti

PEOPLE

The people of the world will never forget the 7.0 earth quake that affected Haitian people. People all over the world are trying to help in so many ways so just when you feel like giving up just say Jesus and the world is there for Haiti.

HAITI WHEN I SAW

When the earth quake hit what I saw on T.V, it touched my heart in ways I did not understand. So I ran out and gave and I can not stop giving to Haiti. Robin is there for you, for everlasting love. This is what I have for Haiti.....

SECOND TIME AROUND

Brings new souls to a closer relationship with God walking and praising God. Always renewing of the mind a change in every thing we do. Now life is different now so all the above is going to help us get on with life a second time around.

FAMILY

Haiti, family is all around you. So if you have lost a loved one, your family now is the family of God. So love them like you would love yours.

FRIEND

You may have been looking for your friends and can't find them. I just want to let you know that God is your friend and you can always find him. He will never let you go

AID

A-All is well for Haiti

I- Increase for the people

D-Determination for salvation under pressure

THINK

Think about the good times that you have had with a loved one or a friend who is not there now. So love, live, smile, laugh, and think about the good times. These things along with your faith are what are going to get you through this.

CHILDREN

Adults, you are going to have to be strong for the children because they are hurting more than you. They are lost and some people is taking advantage of them. So when you see a crying child, confront them with your love and kindness

GLORY

The Master touch will take you to Glory to Glory life that no man can give you .Haiti, you are going to be touched in ways that you are not going to believe. The beauty you are going to see only God can give.

WHAT A NAME

Haiti's nickname is the father land because God put his hands on the land and the people of Haiti and performed miracles .We the people saw new miracles only God could do When we saw people that were under fallen building for ten days or more and they were still alive, only God could do this. Thank you Jesus for saving Haiti

LOVE FOR HAITI

HAITI THE PEOPLE ALL AROUND THE WORLD LOVE HAITI

There is going to be screaming, crying, voices and dreams. But through prayer and love from the people, we as a family will get through this together. No matter how long it takes, remember God is love and we love you Haiti.

GRACE

Haiti, the Lord is going to restore your soul as you walk through the valley of the shadow of death. God's grace and mercy shall follow you all the days of your life.

VICTORY

V-Vision to see again

I-Identity to be restored

C-Concern and love for the people of Haiti

T-Together as one

O-Obedience to God's will

R-Revel in and out of the storm

Y-Years of prophets

REJOICE

Haiti, we will gather together all over the world and rejoice in the new land and be happy with the blessings from God for ever and ever.

Printed in the United States
by Baker & Taylor Publisher Services